my first words
doodle dogs

BUTTERFLY

BIRD

BALL

TOY

BEANIE

SCARF

BOOTS

BACKPACK

LOVE

FRIENDS

HAT

BOWTIE

CHAIR

PILLOW

GLASSES

BOOK

EAT

DRINK

BUCKET

SHOVEL

SIT

WALK

SLEEP

BED

TREE

FLOWER

WET

DRY

DIRTY

CLEAN

HAPPY

SAD

PLAY

DIG

UP

DOWN

HUG

CUDDLE

SMALL & BIG

PAW

Made in the USA
Columbia, SC
21 July 2025